THE CRY OF THE SEAGULL:

JANINE'S SEA OF EMOTIONS

THE CRY OF THE SEAGULL:
JANINE'S SEA OF EMOTIONS

Written and Illustrated by

Janine Hamel Lettera

COPYRIGHT © 2023 Janine Hamel Lettera

All rights reserved.

No part of this book may be reproduced by any mechanical, photographic, or electronic process; nor it may be stored in a retrieval system, transmitted, or otherwise copied for public or private use – other than "fair use" as brief quotations embodied in articles and reviews without prior permission of the author or publisher.

ISBN-978-1-736977682

Printed in the United States of America

Published by: SJF Communications
https://sjfcommunications.com
INFO: sjfcommunications@gmail.com

DEDICATION

This book was put together in the memory of Janine Hamel Lettera who passed away at age 40 in 1999.

It is dedicated to Janine's loving Mom Carol DeVito, Janine's sister Cindy Sevier, and Jenna Lynn and John Richard Sevier, the niece and nephew that Janine never had the pleasure of meeting.

Special thanks go to Susan J. Farese, SJF Communications for editing, formatting, and publishing the book.

"Don't walk in front of me, I may not follow.

Don't walk behind me, I may not lead.

Just walk beside me and be my friend"

Janine Ann Hamel

Table of Contents

LOVE 1
SEA RECOLLECTION (ILLUSTRATION) 2
SEA RECOLLECTION 3
UNTITLED #1 4
FIRE OF LOVE 6
UNTITLED # 2 8
UNTITLED #3 9
UNTITLED #4 10
UNTITLED #5 11
SAND CASTLES, SIDE BY SIDE AND LOVE IS A WARM GLOW (ILLUSTRATION) 12
SAND CASTLES, SIDE BY SIDE AND LOVE IS A WARM GLOW 13
SAND CASTLES 13
SIDE BY SIDE 14
LOVE IS A WARM GLOW 14
BREAKING UP 15
TOGETHER (ILLUSTRATION) 16
TOGETHER 17
UNTITLED #6 18
UNTITLED #7 19
A MEMORY (ILLUSTRATION) 20
A MEMORY 21
UNTITLED #8 22
NATURE 23
OVERHEAD (ILLUSTRATION) 24
OVERHEAD 25
NATURE IS WONDERFUL - SOMETIMES 26
UNTITLED #9 27
UNTITLED # 10 28

A SUNSET (ILLUSTRATION)	29
A SUNSET	30
SEAGULL FLY	31
AUTUMN FALLS (ILLUSTRATION)	33
AUTUMN FALLS	34
A VIVID IMAGINATION	35
LOSS, DEATH AND GRIEF	36
WONDERING (ILLUSTRATION)	37
WONDERING	38
UNTITLED #11	39
IN MEMORY	41
UNTITLED #12	42
HOPE	44
TO ROSE	45
UNTITLED #13	46
PEOPLE	47
UNTITLED #14	48
UNTITLED #15	49
KINDERGARTEN	50
MOM	51
HAPPY MOTHER'S DAY	52
I LOVE YOU	53
MOTHER'S DAY	54
HAPPY THANKSGIVING	55
THANKSGIVING POEM	56
CHRISTMAS	57
TRIBUTE TO MY BEST PAL JANINE BY BARBARA SMITH	59

LOVE

SEA RECOLLECTION (ILLUSTRATION)

SEA RECOLLECTION

When you love someone
You always want to be,
The closest thing to his mind
And not lost out to sea.

You want to be near him
As much as you can,
You want to run away with him
Along the golden sand.

To hear the waves
Crash against the rocks
While he and I stand.
On our special spot.

To see the sun behind the clouds
To hear the gentle breeze blow,
To feel the cold ocean sea
Come up and touch your toes.

To let your hair blow freely
And his as much the same,
Also to hear his tender voice
Just call out your name.

The smile upon your face
Brought happiness to mine,
But I think all we'll ever need
Is just a little more time.

UNTITLED #1

You gave to me your feelings
Your energy your support-
You gave me a reason for living
In a time that was so short.

I still can remember the smile
You shone to me that day-
And in return to you
I turned and walked away-

Maybe I felt something I never did before
And thought it best then, not to open the door-

It could have been the wrong thing
To do at the time
But maybe if I did,
there'd be nothing left to find.

It was such a beautiful thing
To feel protected and secure
But like a bird's broken wing
There is no hope or cure.
You'll go your way, and I'll go mine
And someday we'll meet again
Then the beginning is just saying hi-

But I felt for you once
A very long time ago

It can't happen twice
This I've come to know.

I know I haven't shown
The feelings I have inside
To someone who is so dear to me
That sometimes I can cry.

I may not have a Father
But I really feel I do,
For I've found someone to love
And this man I know is you.

FIRE OF LOVE

A fire was started
In the beginning
It lasted.

It was kindled
By me
And by you

A breeze formed
But blew over
Then…

A gust of wind
Blew out
The fire.

A light was lit
Again, and again
Now ashes.

Smoke rose to
The sky above
A message was sent

Rain fell upon us
And washed away
Our tears

The sun appeared
On the horizon
Didn't stay for long.

It's up to me and you
To make it last
So…

Rebuild the fire
With wood
And keep it burning.

You and I can make
The most
Beautiful fire together.

UNTITLED # 2

Why do I love you?

Is it because of your smile all the time-

or is it because you are mine?

UNTITLED #3

Tomorrow brings
The sun

Along with memories
Of the night before

And all the things
We've done in the past
Are remembered once more.

I'll never forget
Your very first kiss
Your first warm embrace

So tomorrow come quick
So a new day can add to our relationship.

UNTITLED #4

Caring for someone is something you must be sure of.
For if you're not, it's a waste of time.

The minutes, the days, the hours seem endless waiting for a simple hello – and at times a hello just isn't enough- you need just a little bit more-to satisfy the emptiness felt deep within the heart.

On occasion words seem to come out wrong –
when a smile is all you need
and a simple gleam in someone's eye means everything to me.

It's hard to understand someone when they aren't sure of themselves,
but you know someday they will, and love will have just begun.

Because of my feelings I feel for this someone, I've come to realize –
that I myself am incomplete without this other one.

I know things take time and this I must understand, for if I don't soon – I will lose my pains of sand. These grains of sand are memories left deep within my mind-
And one good strong wind will scatter them sky high and then I'll have nothing, not a simple memory – for they too would be washed out to sea.

UNTITLED #5

Soft, sweet, untouched
Unspoiled
Stays in my mind
Breeze blows to and fro

In flight
The birds fly
Sun sinking low
A V is formed
in the sky
With the valley below

When the wind blows
The trees whimper
But the sky is so blue
When the streams trickle

I love you
I love you
I love you!

SAND CASTLES, SIDE BY SIDE AND LOVE IS A WARM GLOW (ILLUSTRATION)

SAND CASTLES, SIDE BY SIDE AND LOVE IS A WARM GLOW

SAND CASTLES

Sandcastles in the sand
Stay for awhile
Stay longer, don't go
Stay till the early
Morning rises.

SIDE BY SIDE

The times things went wrong
The times that went right
The times we sat side by side
On that beautiful summer night

LOVE IS A WARM GLOW

Love is a warm glow
Especially when you're with someone
You know…and love.

BREAKING UP

TOGETHER (ILLUSTRATION)

TOGETHER

Both of us together would be.
If not for saying of "I Love Thee"
It stood in the way of many feelings,
But now it's all over, and everything is revealing.

We knew each other for only a few,
But it seemed like forever when I was with you,
We had good times along with the bad,
But I think it's all over and that's what's sad.

The times in the field,
The times in the park,
Have faded away and into the dark;
The smile upon your face brought happiness to mine,
And at that special moment everything was fine.

We held each other tight
On that long cold winter night,
Looking into each other's eyes;
Not knowing what was on the other side.

So the good times we had
Even those that were bad
Will never change the word Love
Which us together always had.

UNTITLED #6

I lie here and think
Of the times we had
Together alone
Together being glad.

I still see your face
As dim as can be
But I don't want you to cry
Over me.

I wish I could see your face
Just once more,
But that would spoil everything
All the more.

It's best we stay away
If that's ok with you,
But I know you want me
And I definitely want you

If we happen to ever meet again
I'd run to your arms and never let loose,
Because I know we'd both go our separate ways.
And forget all those wonderful happy days.

So, as I lie here and think
There's just three simple words in my mind,
And you know those words are "I Love You"

UNTITLED #7

One lonesome night
With the moon and the stars above-
Two people in need of each other-
Afraid to fall in love-

Strangers we were-
Distant paths to be made one-
Two separate lives to become
A journey into the sun-

Together was happiness
Apart was to be loneliness
Yet we knew the day would come
To end our relationship that had just begun-

Do I say I love you
Do I hold it deep inside
For you mean so much to me
And only in you I can confide

It hurts so much to think
That I have to break down and cry
For you are you and I am I
And I have to say goodbye
.

A MEMORY (ILLUSTRATION)

A MEMORY

The evening was so quiet
The night we were set free,
We walked away in silence
Toward the emptiness of trees.

We dared not to look behind,
We knew it could never be
Us together again,
 Is now just a memory.

We gave each other a kiss
As if to say goodbye,
I know I'll always miss,
I know I'll always cry.

We must forget the times we had
We must never tell anyone else,
The way we cared for each other,
The way we both always felt.

So just keep walking straight ahead
And never turn around,
You must be strong, must not cry,
Cause now you're on your own.

UNTITLED #8

Things have been said, this I know
But time continues on
Giving me a very hard blow.

It just doesn't seem fair
At all sometimes
To act the way we do
We play games far too much for me too

And I wish all would come to understand
The past was real
The time now seems wrong
But tomorrow how can I feel what I can't show?

The days seem so promising
Why can't I express my feelings to someone I really want to know?
The expression in your eyes lightened up my life
The me not to let go
But somehow, I can't go on…

NATURE

OVERHEAD (ILLUSTRATION)

OVERHEAD

The cry of a seagull…
Arms spread like angels wings,
His white figure distinct in the sunlight was purity and love.
He was a lost kite drifting in the breeze and his cry was hunger.
As he soared the sun touched sky, the waves began to crash,
The sky darkened.

NATURE IS WONDERFUL - SOMETIMES

The rim of day shades beyond the trees;
Alone, the spacious sky above me turns to night.

A bird drifts across the moonlit shadows,
As the stars give off radiant light.
Suddenly a cool breeze sweeps across my face;

A reflection in the pond startles me;
The sound of water trickles through my mind.

UNTITLED #9

Skimming as a swan in full sail

The light poured and splashed on the white skin
where the last shadows of black had been polished and bleached away

And his mane and tail tossed in thick fine silk like a flurry of snow.

The stallion rose into the sun and leaped into the air…

UNTITLED # 10

Beyond the world that I can see
Is a world beneath the sea
Where the coral seems to glow
Where iridescent waters flow

A SUNSET (ILLUSTRATION)

A SUNSET

Oh sunset, I see you going away,
Please can't you ever stay?
Can't you stay for just awhile,
Just enough to make me smile?

Where do you go behind the trees
What can you do with the summer breeze,
Will you come again real soon?
Before the rising crescent moon?

I guess I'll have to wait,
To see such a beautiful sight,
Even the cool summer breeze,
Won't hurry this long night.

SEAGULL FLY

Overhead, the cry of a seagull caught my attention. His arms spread like angels' wings. His white figure, distinct in the sunlight, gave me a feeling of purity and love.

"Come seagull, don't be afraid." The seagull gently landed on the water's edge.

"Come, please come." His movements were hesitant as he approached.

"Here, seagull. Here's a piece of bread for you."

I reached out my hand hoping he'd reach out his beak in return. Just as he seemed confident that it was alright, I heard another cry overhead. It was another seagull, calling. I looked at the ocean's edge, only to see the seagull land next to the other one. Both stood there with curiosity in their eyes. They had a look of trust and then they took to the sky, flying slowly with their wings barely moving.

At that moment my mother called me to come to dinner. I grabbed my blanket and headed for the house. This was our summer home, and we were only going to stay for another week.

Days passed and every morning I ran to the beach in search of my friend. This continued for days. Each day the seagull trusted me more. Never did he come and take the bread from my hand but I just knew someday he would.

The day came when I had to say goodbye. While my Mother and Father loaded the car, I ran to the beach hoping the seagull would come to me that last day. The seagull was there as every day before. I reached out my hand and prayed. He moved closer and tilted his head and looked at me. Just as he was within reach of my leg, a cry overhead took his attention.

He walked toward the water and then stopped. He turned and looked at me as if he knew it was time to say goodbye and then he took to the sky.

As I stared at the two of them heading toward the horizon, a thought came over me. The seagull was like me in many ways.

AUTUMN FALLS (ILLUSTRATION)

AUTUMN FALLS

Autumn leaves falling on the ground
They fall so soft they make no sound,
Wind blows them to and fro,
Not knowing where to go.

And the sun sets beyond the clouds,
Revealing hidden shadows on the ground,
And the branches on the trees look so bare,
Against the blackening mist of night air.

Children running through the leaves,
Scattering them with nearly ease,
They jump in piles ten feet high,
It looks as though they can touch the sky.

Snow drifting down from the sky,
They pass each other by and by,
Covering the ground of fallen leaves,
Leaving the emptiness of the trees.

A VIVID IMAGINATION

Across the placid waters, a brilliant tinge caught my eye. The trees whispered toward the iridescent water. In the distance, a line, so perfectly straight, extended infinitely. Above were rows of tufted cotton lingering in an enchanting sky. They cast darkness below, but rays of light broke through. It looked as though the sky was burning fire, scattering luminous rays upon everything within reach.

It gave me a sense of imagination, which was a feeling of warmth. The array of colors slowly ran together like children's tears on sorrowful red faces.

The reflections in my mind left me glad to see such a vivid sunset.

LOSS, DEATH AND GRIEF

WONDERING (ILLUSTRATION)

WONDERING

Sun sets beyond the trees,
Air is filled with a cool breeze,
Everything glistens from the new fallen snow
But where it came from no one will ever know.

Is there a place called Heaven,
Where clouds have numbers through eleven,
Where everything is always bright,
Even angels dress in white?

Where there's only one way in,
And no way ever out,
Where sounds are so quiet,
Everything is beautiful in sight.

We'll never know till the day
The man up there takes us away.

UNTITLED #11

I dreamed I saw a moonlit stair
Twisting, winding infinitely
Leading for man, a path,
Into the land of eternity.

Halfway up, I started to climb,
When a man came up to me,
With empty eyes he gazed
And asked, "who may I be".

I am someone you will fear
As you journey on,
And before you are aware,
I will come, my son.

I am great and powerful,
And your life is in my hands,
I am death, my child
"Do you understand?"

Yes, I understand Sir,
But you will not stop me
I am too determined
To reach prosperity.

"Death will come, my child,
Before you are aware,

You'll never reach this Heaven
And the wrenching moonlit stair."

No that cannot happen
At least not to me,
I am too determined
To reach prosperity.

IN MEMORY

When February comes along
A certain feeling, I get
Memories of days are lost
And everything I forget.

Nothing will ever be again
That I understand
But do you know how much
I wish it never began.

The day was long and short
However, you may see
But anything that I see
Brings back certain memories

I knew for all my life
Which now is only 16
But when you went away
I was just a beginning teen.

Mom knows as much as I
That you loved her so.
Why – do I ask every day?
Why…you had to go.

UNTITLED #12

I dreamed I saw, on a moonlit stair
Spreading his hands on the multitude there,
A man who cried for love gone stale,
And ice-cold hearts to tell our tale.

I watched as fear took the old man's gaze,
Hopes of the young in troubled graves
I see no day I heard him say,
Of people seeing light of day.

He told of death as a bone white haze,
Fate too late all wretches run
And hate in the lives of everyone.

From Mother's love is the son estranged
Married by his precious gain,
The Earth will shake in two will break,
And death all around it will take.

Flee for your life who heard me say,
Fear for your time, count your day,
Let all your treasure make you,
For the fires of Hell will take you.

People of the Earth listen to the wise man,
Reach out, take his hand.
Beware the storm that gathers here,

For in your hearts, you know it's fear.
Awake to the new life, take my hand,
Fly and find a new green land,
The answer is that of love,
Return like the pure white dove.

Children of the world
Please listen to me!
The vision fades, a voice I hear,
But still I fear, this voice inside
Listen!

HOPE

TO ROSE

Today is to fulfill the dreams of tomorrow
Tomorrow is but a memory of yesterday
Yesterday is all but a past experience…of time

For time itself is precious
For time will tell all things…
Great and small.

Love you,
Janine

UNTITLED #13

In a world
I am.

A world of hatred?
No.

A world of love?
No.

A different world?
Yes.

A world like shining armor,
Where everyone is free.
Away from hatred, love and war
In a place…just me

Where trees are full of fantasy,
And the sky is deep blue green,
Crystal lakes gleam in the light,
And nothing called the night.

In a world,
I am.

A different world?
Yes.

PEOPLE

UNTITLED #14

See the funny little man
Standing in the rain,
Holding his hands,
As if he were ashamed.

Ashamed of his shabby clothes,
Or maybe his worn-out shoes,
Even his wrinkled old face
Or his hair, gray and old.

Who are you little man?
Please tell me your name,
What are you doing here
In the midst of the morning rain?

Where did you come from,
Who do you know?
Do you have anyone,
Or isn't it so?

Why am I thinking
All these funny thoughts
He's a man, alone and happy
Why don't I just leave him alone?

UNTITLED #15

The weeping child,
Tears trickled,
His eyes red
Sadness appeared
His nose wet,
Water running.
His mouth open,
Crying, crying

KINDERGARTEN

Another year has come to an end
Like flowers we grew and made a new friend.
We learned our letters and numbers on sight,
We also found out wrong from right,
We did so many wonderful things,
We're waiting to see what next year brings,
We're sorry to say goodbye in June,
But will be back and in full bloom!

MOM

HAPPY MOTHER'S DAY

A thing of beauty is a joy forever – It's loveliness increases – A Mother is an ornament of love, with many words of wisdom – understanding comes naturally along with patience and grace. A permanent statue to live by and be always proud to follow.

You've given me courage, strength and femininity – all of what are you – so on this special day I say – There's no one loved more than you.

I LOVE YOU

Though we may be miles apart,
You're always with me and in my heart,
Your thoughts are there from day to day,
There is so much I want to say,

But I think you know, how I feel inside
For you're the best Mother and friend,
There could ever be.

Love always,
Jeanine

MOTHER'S DAY

Mom,
We'll always have a Mommy,
A mother, a friend,
Someone you can count on,
And always depend…

On little things that make you want to cry
And sometimes wish you'd want to die…

Of love you will always see,
That's our love, Cindy and me…

To you it's all been known well
That Mom you're the greatest that we all can tell…

To everyone around us,
We can always fuss,
And cherish that you're one
And you belong to us!

Love always,
Janine and Cindy

HAPPY THANKSGIVING

Here's a little something
To let you know I care
I had no time for anything
Except this tiny prayer:

Dear Lord

On this special holiday
No different form the rest,
May we all be happy,
And always be at our best.

Let us all be cheerful,
When trouble does arise,
For time passes quickly
Right in front of our eyes.

THANKSGIVING POEM

I couldn't find a card with loving words to say
What I feel in my heart…on this special day.

I'm growing up, as you can see
Remembering thoughts which used to be.

Daddy's gone as we both see
But life goes on indefinitely.

Tomorrow's no different than the day before
I just wish time was a little more.

Things I've said in the past using a witty tongue,
Have come and gone through the days having only fun.

Time will never slow down
And I hope you'll see
That I love you very much
And I always will.

Happy Thanksgiving,
Love, Janine

CHRISTMAS

One light shines
        On the edge of a tree
        A star so bright,
                For prosperity,

One bird sits
        A pure white dove
        Representing to the world
                Peace and Love,

One child born
        On Christmas Day
        He's called the "Son of God"
                I heard them say.

But one woman
        Alone in the world stands,
        And that's my Mom
                Who understands,

She will bring,
        Us strength to carry on,
        Giving, with very much love and care,
                And I know - She'll always be there.

TRIBUTE TO MY BEST PAL JANINE

BY BARBARA SMITH

My pal Janine was my best friend since we were in the seventh grade. We were like sisters growing up and it was awesome to have such a special friend in my life. We supported each other through thick and thin and did crazy things together. She lost her father and grandfather within a year of each other at a young age. She loved to write but was very private about what she wrote. We were very into music growing up. She played guitar and the organ and I played the flute and we loved to sing. We both went to college to become teachers and she pursued her teaching career and I took a different path. I moved to California in my late twenties and we still remained close. Janine unfortunately got cancer and passed away at the young age of 40. This was a very rough time for all of us. She is always in my heart and I think of what could have been. Until we meet again.

Following is a Tribute I wrote for Janine:

Tribute to My Best Pal Janine – Written by Barbara Smith

Janine and I were pals from the grade of seven but now she's gone and lives in Heaven.

She lost her father and her Pop-Pop at a young age. Writing her thoughts helped her to turn the page.

Between, Janine, her Mother and Cindy there was much love. For each other they always went beyond and above.

Her mother Carol did a great job as a single mother until she met Jim who became her significant other. To Janine and Cindy he became a dad and he treated them with respect for which they were glad.

She came from a big family with many cousins. They had lots of parties by the dozens.

We did crazy things when we were young - played guitar and flute and many songs were sung. We loved to dress for Halloween there were no better times that we had seen.

She loved Steely Dan and the Moody Blues. In her eyes no one could fill their shoes.

We played in a bar softball league, sometimes in games it would cause fatigue. Janine was a pitcher and played shortstop in most of the games she was at the top.

She met Frank at the Jersey Shore and he then became her forevermore. They had a great house and lived a good life. He was a good husband and she a good wife.

She pursued and earned a teaching degree. There was no other career that she wanted to be. She was so good at what she did everyone she taught was a lucky kid.

Then came the day Janine became ill, it wasn't as simple as taking a pill. She was a trooper and fought a good fight but her soul was about to take flight.

One day in May when the end was near her father came and she went without fear. He brought her home to Heaven above, never to be broken, the everlasting love.

Janine you are always in my heart, until the day that I do part. Thinking of you until the end, until we meet again my friend.

Your Forever Pal, Barbara

www.ingramcontent.com/pod-product-compliance
Lightning Source LLC
Chambersburg PA
CBHW071030080526
44587CB00015B/2561